fifi lapin

The Wonderful World of
Fifi Lapin

Style Secrets from a Furry Fashionista

CHRONICLE BOOKS
SAN FRANCISCO

First published in the United States in 2012 by Chronicle Books LLC.
First published in the United Kingdom in 2010 by Hodder & Stoughton.

Copyright © 2010 by Fifi Lapin.

Library of Congress Cataloging-in-Publication Data:

Lapin, Fifi.
The wonderful world of Fifi Lapin : style secrets from a furry fashionista / Fifi Lapin.
p. cm.
ISBN 978-1-4521-0808-7
1. Fashion design. 2. Fashion designers. 3. Women's clothing. I. Title.

TT507.L275 2012
746.9'2—dc23

2011025897

Manufactured in China
Cover Design by Ayako Akazawa

1 3 5 7 9 10 8 6 4 2

Chronicle Books LLC
680 Second Street
San Francisco, California 94107
www.chroniclebooks.com

For Sonny Hare

F.L.

Contents

Introduction

Hello. I'm Fifi Lapin, and I'm a fashionholic . . .

While my friends were dreaming about a world made of grass and carrots, I knew that true happiness resided in a well-stocked wardrobe. Inevitably, my mother is to blame. I remember gazing up at her in awe from my playpen as she fixed her sparkly earrings that went perfectly with her polished shoes before she hopped over to the dressing table to pick up the matching clutch bag. As I got older I would steal a spritz of her Chanel No. 5 and desperately push tissue into the ends of her Jimmy Choos just so that I could catwalk along the edge of the window seat imagining I was one of those long-legged beauties I'd seen in her glossy copies of *Vogue*. Given fashion was so clearly imprinted in my DNA, it's perhaps no surprise that I find myself thinking about Mulberry's Alexa bag while I'm brushing my teeth or Louis Vuitton bunny ears while out walking Stella, my dog. Sometimes these visions can take me quite by surprise—last week I was talking to my accountant and, as I looked up from my iPhone (modern technology can be so distracting), I realized he'd turned into a very fabulous jewel-encrusted swallow-print Miu Miu heel.

A couple of years ago, I began a blog about my wildly fashionable life. As I took a front-row seat at fashion shows around the globe, scoured countless magazines and look books, and people-watched the days away, my admiration for our talented designers grew and my personal style stature developed to such a degree that *Elle* dubbed me "the world's most stylish bunny"—a hotly contested title, let me tell you. And then my darling editor called and asked if I would consider sharing the wealth of knowledge I had gleaned after hours of collating and curating my hat, shoe, scarf, bag, dress, trouser, shirt, and jacket collection with you, the reader. How could I refuse?

As my favorite subject aside from fashion is myself, in the coming pages I'm going to talk you through a few of my own wardrobe dilemmas. These are situations that I'm sure you've probably experienced in your own life—like what to wear when you're whisked off on a romantic date with barely a moment's notice, how to do casual without looking like a slob, and how to make it impossible for anyone to refuse to give you what you really want. Sound familiar? Thought so . . .

I might be a trust-fund bunny, but at heart I'm just your average rabbit. So, while all the outfits I'm modeling are high-end designer, no need to worry—it doesn't matter if your allowance won't stretch to that fresh-from-the-runway Dior frock. You can learn a lot from the designers (they are the experts after all) and bring that knowledge to wherever you happen to shop. Main Street is rightly famous for its fast turnaround of catwalk-inspired clothes, and vintage is very accessible right now, so I hope my little book will inspire you to break out of your safety zone and get creative. Plus, thanks to the wonderful partnerships between the designers and retailers that have become so à la mode recently, it's easy to get a little bit of Stella McCartney at a non-stellar price. And don't forget accessories; they can really make an outfit pop. Some say real estate is the best investment, but I say you'll never regret the money you've spent on a good-quality handbag.

Style is not just your attire; it's your attitude. Stay true to yourself, wear what you like, and wear it with pride. When it comes to being stylish, there are no hard-and-fast rules. Clothes are there to keep us warm and to stop us from showing more than is proper to the man on the bus, but fashion is there to make us feel fabulous. This book is about celebrating the joyful adventure that is getting dressed, so have fun with fashion, and you'll be just like me!

bunny kisses
fifi lapin
xxx

MONDAY

Style Bunny

*Or, how to look fluffy and
stylish every day of the week . . .*

Peter Som

Monday

Why don't you like Mondays? I absolutely love them. When I stand in front of my wardrobe contemplating the week ahead, I often think of the Great American Novelist Mark Twain (and you thought this was a shallow book about fashion, shame on you!). Twain said, "The finest clothing made is a person's skin, but, of course, society demands something more than this." My personal philosophy is never disappoint society. Today society is my best friend, Ruby Gatta. We're having lunch, and I need to strike the right balance between relaxed and chic.

Fifi's TIPS *for Everyday Style . . .*

⭐ Learn from the masters. Decide who your favorite designers are and follow them over the seasons.

⭐ Express your personality. Style comes from within, so don't be afraid to be unique.

⭐ Make the most of your figure. Whether you have gorgeously delicate ankles or a beautifully sculptured décolletage, highlight your assets! See below for more tips.

⭐ Appreciate timeless essentials. A simple white T-shirt, a beautifully cut blazer, a perfectly fitting pair of jeans are all classics. Once you have the basics right, you can layer on the trends.

⭐ Wear what you feel good in. Great outfit + feeling good = confidence = always looking stylish. Now why don't they teach you equations like that at school?

PETITE If you have a nicely shaped pair of gams, a shorter skirt can lengthen the legs. Belt up on your natural waistline or above to create even more length. Drop waists (below the hip) should be avoided at all costs.

BOYISH Add feminine touches to your basics with pretty detailing like frills and bows. Mix soft and hard fabrics to soften while adding definition. A V-neck is handy for boosting the bustline.

HOURGLASS A cinched-in waist never fails to flatter and will give your body definition. Go for tailored pieces that will follow your curves rather than mask them.

FULLER FIGURE Think simple and sleek. Baggy clothes will only add volume. Don't be scared to wear fitted clothes—straight flat-fronted skirts and trousers will give you length, and wrap dresses will hug you in all the right places.

COVER UP A key factor to successful everyday style is to think from the outside in. Before you start worrying about what's going on underneath, make sure you have the perfect coat. Really, what is the use of slaving over a hot wardrobe only to grab a practical anorak or a too-short jacket on your way out the door? It will take some serious work to undo the impression of being someone who doesn't think things through.

Burberry always says simple chic; the trench is my number one basic.

Burberry

Givenchy

Marni

Céline

SIMPLY CHIC It's hard to think of little old *moi* as a minimalist, but sometimes I like to clear my head with a clean line or two. My mother, who would never have a hair out of place, taught me that to make a simple look sing, you must ensure that your hair and makeup are also simple—by which she meant simply perfect.

Givenchy. Audrey Hepburn's wardrobe both professionally and personally was almost exclusively Givenchy. What more of an incentive do I need to choose this iconic brand? The strong shape combined with monochrome shades makes a striking statement. Black can be a bunny's best friend, but roomy pocketed pants aren't necessarily for more well-endowed thighs like mine. The horizontal stripes do help to balance the look though, so it could be a winner.

Marni. I also like to pair simple, clean shapes with bold color for instant impact. This confident red is great for cheering the mood and is so effectively paired with the complimentary colors of coffee and pink. Don't forget to match up your accessories.

Céline. Phoebe Philo, protégée of Stella McCartney and formerly of Chloé, weaves her magic touch into the Céline label with this incredibly simple yet stylish ensemble. It works so beautifully because everything is the same toffee tone, even down to the model's polished skin and swept-back hair. Unfortunately, with my snowy pallor, I could look a bit washed out, and I don't want Ruby insisting we go on another exclusively beet juice detox.

*U*pdate an old shirt by replacing plain buttons with something more unusual.

FANTASTIC FABRIC Once you're feeling more confident and you've found out what suits you in terms of shape and fit, you can add some oomph with print and texture.

Marni. This eclectic look will show off my creative side. I love the tights, though I am thankful for the platform heels as patterned legs aren't always so flattering. The mixture of textures and the exotic choice of fabrics hint at my love of travel, and paired with the cute bangles I picked up in Bali, it's the perfect excuse for bringing up my truly fascinating holiday stories.

Balenciaga

Marni

Balenciaga. If you fall head over paws for a really bold print like this gorgeous little Balenciaga number, play it simple by keeping the print to the top half of your frame and going for bare legs or opaque tights. Of course, I can pull off the matching gladiator boots, but be wary, this outfit works because über-talented head designer Nicolas Ghesquière put it together. For mere mortals, I would suggest making just one statement per outfit.

JAZZ IT UP I like to think I know how to express my personality through my choice of clothes, and what a personality it is. Just follow your heart and forget what's appropriate or safe; just have fun!

Wrap up your hair with bows for a cute look.

Throw on some specs for a quirky, studious style.

Be confident with color.

High-waisted shorts lengthen the leg; add a belt at the waist for a flattering shape.

A giant pussy bow and Jesus sandals mismatch perfectly.

Grandpa was surprised when I plucked these specs off his nose, but as I explained, vintage is all the rage these days.

Colorful stripes reflect my love of candy canes!

Adding a geometric pattern to an otherwise simple outfit can really make an impact—though to be honest, everything is a little blurry.

Marc by Marc Jacobs

Paul Smith

3.1 Phillip Lim

FIFI'S 10 MOST USEFUL ACCESSORIES YOU WILL EVER OWN . . .

1. *A cocktail ring. A great conversation starter. Especially if yours is a family heirloom from the Watership Down dynasty.*

2. *A clutch. For evening glam, you can't just carry any old bag. Make it a sparkler for added va-va-voom.*

3. *A gold necklace with a simple pendant. Or silver if you prefer. Make the pendant something small and classic—a tiny bird, a small heart, or a single diamond—for a chic look.*

4. *A classic watch. Gold or silver, slim, and dainty. These are the watchwords for an elegant timepiece.*

5. *A belt. A flattering addition to your wardrobe. Never underestimate the power of cinching in your waistline to create the classic hourglass shape.*

6. *Fabulous sunglasses. Even if you don't need to hide your dark circles from the paparazzi à la moi, you will always feel like a superstar wearing a giant pair of designer sunnies.*

7. *Flats. Whatever happens to be on trend, be it ballet slippers, smart brogues, or jazz shoes, a practical pair of fashionable flats will never let down a carefully considered outfit.*

8. *A bangle. A great way to add a pop of color. There are lots of stunning vintage examples out there. Glass, wood, or enameled are perfect; if it's made of bakelite, it's allowed, but ditch anything made of cheap plastic.*

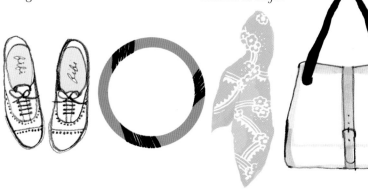

9. *A scarf. The right one can add a touch of cool to an outfit, but don't just tie it at the neck. A headscarf and huge shades will let you live out those movie starlet daydreams, or just attach it to your bag strap to add a spot of color to an outfit.*

10. *A leather day bag. Splash out what you can on this investment piece. A great-quality leather bag will stand the test of time in the style stakes and will only look better with age. It's not often you get to say that.*

* A copy of Vogue *should also always be on hand.*

DOGGY STYLE

I love Stella au naturel, so I do err on the side of caution when choosing clothing for her. My top tip is to avoid miniature versions of clothing we would wear. When I see dogs wearing tiny hoodies and miniature leather jackets, I think it looks odd (rabbits are a whole different ball game). So think practical with a twist. That's why I love Stella's Mulberry raincoat with its stylish red trim, and Stella loves it, too. She absolutely hates getting wet, and I don't like seeing her unhappy, though I do draw the line at canine Wellingtons! For the ultimate in doggy chic, I've coordinated our outfits; it's so easy—just pick out the main colors and don't forget to accessorize!

What shall I wear today?

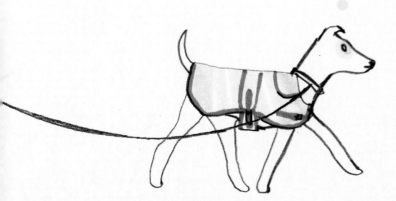

> *I am so indecisive. I just couldn't decide what to wear. . . . Time to call in an expert!*

Eley Kishimoto

How can you not love a company whose mission statement is to make the world a prettier place? Eley Kishimoto (Mark Eley and Wakako Kishimoto) are a husband and wife dream-team who work out of a former jam factory in South London. They began their careers as textile designers for hire, but in 1996—after their patterns had graced the clothes of Hussein Chalayan, Marc Jacobs, and Alexander McQueen—they launched their first collection. Their guiding principle is one of art rather than fashion and no one else could make pop sox so hot!

FL. *How would you describe the girl who chooses to wear Eley Kishimoto?*

ME. A girl that knows a thing or two.
WK. A girl who follows her instinct rather than fashion.

FL. *You're hailed the "patron saints of print." Do you see yourselves as printmakers first and fashion designers second—or the other way 'round?*

ME. We are designers in the general sense; we specialize in print for sure and are primarily using fashion to expose this. We work in many other mediums and are open to reinterpreting our ideology, which is that we are surface decorators and the world has many surfaces to cover.
WK. It all starts as some tingling "feeling" and often both elements are mentally developed together, so I don't know which comes first or second. But I know prints are our trademark, like draping is to some others. We always consider prints as an integral part of our fashion collections.

FL. Your collections reference everything from fairy tales (Dark Wood Wander A/W '05–'06) to '60s airline stewardesses (Jet Set Masala A/W '09–'10). At what stage of the collection do you conceive the concept and name?

WK. The concept or story is there from the beginning, following the "feeling" I mentioned. The name comes much later, when we feel the work is almost completed. It seems to me that by the act of naming a collection, it is no longer just yours; it somehow gains a kind of independence from you.

FL. You spend a lot of time traveling to glamorous locations around the globe and have showrooms in London, Paris, Japan, and Scandinavia. Where do you feel most at home and why?

ME. At home in Brixton in our kitchen cooking with our children around—Wakako is knitting or gardening with a glass of wine. There's no pressure from work or any impending travel plans.
WK. Our home in London. It is not so much that I feel I belong there; it is more like I feel it belongs to me.

FL. Your prints have appeared on a multitude of items from cars and Frisbees to furniture and sculptures. If you could put your print on anything in the world, what would it be and why?

ME. We're still open to anything. The possibility of printing on the surface of water in a clean way would be interesting.

FL. *Your designs always seem to exude happiness. Do you consider yourselves optimists? What makes you really smile?*

ME. Everyday life, bad jokes, other people's laughter, good food, good wine, stupid television, being naughty, going fast, winning a bet, embarrassing oneself in any way, other people's creativity, joie de vivre.

WK. We are happy to have a lifestyle that combines work and family, and every day we strive for joy; even if it is hard work, it is our work, which is a gift.

FL. *It's clear I'm passionate about fashion. Tell me about your latest passion.*

ME. Motorbike flat track racing and always chocolate and milk. I am also on a mission to find the best vanilla milk shake as I travel around the world. It's pure simplicity, but done well, it can be magical.

WK. I bought a random flower bulb from a market store a while ago. I don't know what I was thinking. I have never been a domestic person, never mind being green-fingered. Though I often draw plants, I know nothing about them. After about two weeks of being buried in the soil, this green thing peeped its head! I guess that's what plants do, but I was very chuffed. It is now about two feet tall, and I am determined to see it flower (according to the label, it is called a dahlia).

FL. *What is "style" to you?*

ME. Something that someone has naturally without making any effort.

WK. The state where a common commodity becomes no longer common in the ownership of a person and renders individual personality to him or her.

FL. *Oh, just one last question. I'm off to meet my friend Ruby for a lunch date and want to look effortlessly cool. What shall I wear today?*

ME. What do you think of this one?

WK. It needs no effort at all.

Cool and cute—perfect!
bunny kisses
fifi lapin
xxx

TUESDAY
Hangin' Loose

Or, how to dress down but not out . . .

Karen Walker

Tuesday

I'm having a lazy day today. Mainly, I'll be lounging around my town house, but that's no excuse to look sloppy. I'm expecting a delivery . . . yes, one of the fifty bicycles Lagerfeld has made for Chanel should be arriving any moment. I'm thinking our first meeting (the bicycle and I) should be commemorated with effortlessly dressed-down cool. And I still have to walk my faithful hound—you never know, I might be papped from the bushes!

Fifi's TIPS *for Being a Jean-ius*

Jeans have become .part of our daily uniform, so don't you dare shirk on finding the perfect pair. You may have to try on a lot of pairs to find "the one"—the magic pair that pull in your tum, lift your tush, and lengthen your legs to heaven—but when you do, it will be so satisfying you'll want to buy three pairs!

JEGGINGS Jeans meet leggings to create a sprayed-on effect. Should be reserved for the very young, and even then a long top is advisable to avoid the panty-hose look.

SKINNY Super-fashionable skinnies can give you instant cool. You don't necessarily have to be skinny to wear them, but a word of warning; too tight around the waist, and your tummy will have to go somewhere—veto anything that leaves you spilling out the edges. Choose a mid- to high-rise—too low and you'll be showing off more rear than you intended.

STRAIGHT The classic jean that suits most figures. The long, slim shape will give a leaner look, and a generous rise will lift your derrière. Go for a traditional deep-blue rinse and consider ironing in a press line for a polished look.

BOOT CUT A slim cut with a slim flare can balance out pear-shaped gals. Wear long with heels to really lengthen those legs. Be careful not to stray into bell-bottom territory though; costume is always so last season.

BOYFRIEND Style legend Coco Chanel, my icon and muse, championed masculine trousers as a key staple of the modern woman's wardrobe. Worn with a carefree confidence, low-slung wide-legged jeans can ooze sex appeal. Coco would have added a striped tee, but remember to tuck it in or keep it lean to create shape. For easy-peasy chic, roll up the bottoms just above the ankle and pair with smart brogues.

HIGH WAISTED Whether small or large, you need to have a well-balanced body shape to work this look. A flattish stomach also helps. Try a belt to exaggerate the style and wear with a higher heel to elongate the leg.

CROPPED A good option for summer, these can dramatically shorten the leg, so be careful if you're petite. Heels are tempting but can look tacky. Try a classic ballet pump for a cute '50s take.

ROCKIN' RABBIT If you spied me in this outfit, at first glance you would definitely think rock-star chic, but look closer and you will see it's altogether more practical. The combination of slinky leggings and oversized jacket with 101 practical pockets gives a relaxed yet flattering silhouette, while the racoon tail speaks of adventure.

Practically cool...

William Rast

3.1 Phillip Lim

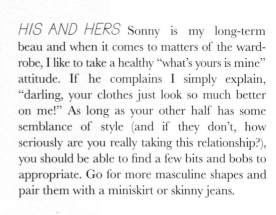

Cynthia Rowley

HIS AND HERS Sonny is my long-term beau and when it comes to matters of the wardrobe, I like to take a healthy "what's yours is mine" attitude. If he complains I simply explain, "darling, your clothes just look so much better on me!" As long as your other half has some semblance of style (and if they don't, how seriously are you really taking this relationship?), you should be able to find a few bits and bobs to appropriate. Go for more masculine shapes and pair them with a miniskirt or skinny jeans.

3.1 Phillip Lim. Re-create this gorgeous summer look by chucking your other half's linen suit in the washing machine with a couple of red socks. You don't even need to add a new hole to his belt, just loop it 'round for an instant style statement.

Cynthia Rowley. This is a wonderful example of how this mix 'n' match approach can work. Clever styling means this oversized blazer doesn't swamp my tiny frame. The block color allows the pieces to work together beautifully. The V-neck tee shows off a bit of skin and is tucked into the skirt allowing for definition. Clean, strong tailoring against girly sparkle from the skirt finish the look. It may be a little short for a bicycle though. . . .

Layer jackets and coats for a quirky yet practical look.

HAPPY DAYS Thank god for the day dress! Many is the morning when I've gotten up late, can't think what to wear with what, and have five minutes to look fabulous. Even in winter, you can simply throw a style savior (a.k.a. day dress) over a pair of opaque tights, add a cute pair of heels, and you're working a look.

Richard Nicoll. I love this dress for less-confident days. The A-line shape covers up a multitude of sins yet still sings in this gorgeous lilac silk. You could always add a belt if you wanted more definition. Paired with one of my essential accessories, the scarf, you can see how it adds a certain *je ne sais quoi* to the overall impression.

Richard Nicoll

Missoni

Missoni. First launched in the '50s, Missoni's zigzag, multicolored knits captured the imagination of the fashion world and went on to become an iconic signature of the brand. As well as being ever so stylish, a sweater dress is cozy and practical. You could leave off the cigarette pants and just pop it over a pair of gray tights and clompy Chloé heels. I think it looks great either way.

JUST RELAX

I always say we must suffer for our art, but on days like today, comfort is a lovely thing. I hasten to add, this does not mean sweatpants. Have some respect, sisters!

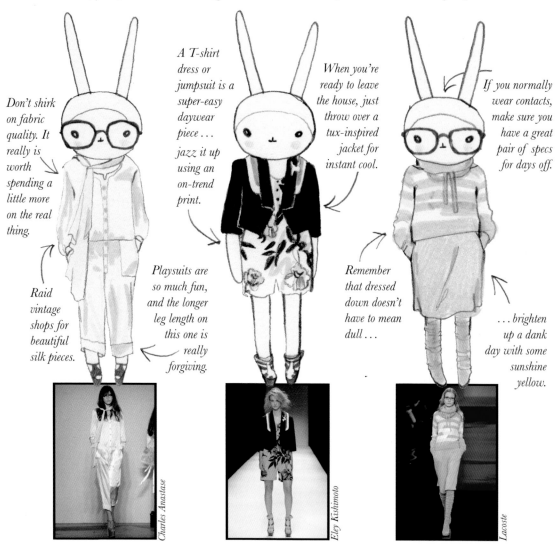

Don't shirk on fabric quality. It really is worth spending a little more on the real thing.

Raid vintage shops for beautiful silk pieces.

A T-shirt dress or jumpsuit is a super-easy daywear piece . . . jazz it up using an on-trend print.

Playsuits are so much fun, and the longer leg length on this one is really forgiving.

When you're ready to leave the house, just throw over a tux-inspired jacket for instant cool.

Remember that dressed down doesn't have to mean dull . . .

If you normally wear contacts, make sure you have a great pair of specs for days off.

. . . brighten up a dank day with some sunshine yellow.

Charles Anastase

Eley Kishimoto

Lacoste

41

Beauty Bunny

Or, how to whip up a delicious face mask . . .

On a day off from shopping, modeling, or going to the opening of an envelope, I like to get my housekeeper Mrs. Fluffy to make me up some of mother's famous carrot face mask. The recipe has been handed down through generations of Lapins, and I swear it's why we all look so youthful. It's fantastic for oily skin and can even help those dreaded wrinkles . . .

1. A lot of the goodness in a delicious carrot is in the skin, so first of all, get a couple of nice organic carrots and give them a good wash. Cut into chunks and pop in a steamer. Cook until soft and then mash until there are no lumps. Science Flash: Carrots can help protect the skin from free radicals and promote the regeneration of healthy skin cells.

2. Stir in 1 tablespoon of natural honey.
Honey is known for its moisturizing properties and is also a natural antiseptic.

3. Mix in 1 tablespoon of olive oil.
Another great moisturizer, olive oil helps keep your skin supple.

4. Squeeze in a few drops of fresh lemon juice.
Lemon is a natural astringent and will help clean greasy skin. The amount of lemon you should add depends on your skin. Add about 6 to 8 drops if your skin is on the dry side. If your skin is more oily, add up to 1 tablespoon.

5. Now carefully stir in enough mineral water to give the mixture a creamy consistency. *Not too much, or your face mask will be runny and mess up your Gucci dressing gown. If the mask is already about right, you may not need to add the water.*

To apply the face mask . . .

Gently wash your face with warm water and pat dry with a fluffy towel. Apply the mask evenly avoiding the delicate eye area. Allow to set for about 15 minutes. Rinse your face and feel refreshed. Now go and find someone to admire your new glowing complexion. Ahhh, there's nothing like a bit of quality Fifi time.

. . . a peek at some of my family snaps.

I ♡ london!

My and Ruby's mums in the '70s.

Me and Ruby on a shopping
trip in Milan.

I'm terribly well traveled . . .

Brrrrr!

Mother and me (I'm about 3 here).

Sonny and me in Paris.

I finally got a good one!

> *I am so indecisive. I just couldn't decide what to wear. . . . Time to call in an expert!*

Emma Hill

THE ENGLISH GIRL FROM THE BIG APPLE, EMMA HILL WORKED AT CALVIN KLEIN, MARC JACOBS, AND GAP BEFORE BECOMING CREATIVE DIRECTOR AT MULBERRY. SHE'S SENT A LITTLE BLACK PUG DOWN THE RUNWAY, SHE'S PUT CAROUSEL HORSES IN STORE WINDOWS, SHE DOESN'T MAKE BAGS THAT WEIGH A TON EVEN BEFORE YOU'VE PUT YOUR ESSENTIALS INSIDE, AND SHE'S GOT A GRANNY KNITTING SWEATERS FOR HER IN SCOTLAND—WHAT A WONDERFULLY PRACTICAL GOOD-TIME GAL.

FL. How would you describe the girl who chooses to wear Mulberry?

EH. The Mulberry girl is someone who is fun, stylish, playful, and chic! I think our shows reflect that—for my first collection, spring/summer 2010, we transformed the library in New York's Soho House into a fairground, complete with carousel horses and thousands of balloons.

Stella loves Mulberry ... See how much on page 27!

FL. You spent thirteen years in New York working for big American companies like Gap and Marc Jacobs—what's it like being back in the U.K. and at the creative helm of such a quintessentially English company as Mulberry?

EH. I loved living and working in New York, but it was so nice to come home to London. The English appreciate eccentricity and have an effortless sense of humor. I have a genuine affinity with Mulberry; that's why I accepted the job! I like people to be able to make our clothes and bags their own—to allow them to function for them. So, you could wear one of our bags over the shoulder or across the body or take the strap off altogether.

FL. Where does the inspiration for a collection come from?

EH. For fall '10 I became obsessed by the movie *Valley of the Dolls*, based on the novel by Jacqueline Susann; naughty English royalty, and leopards! You can see the motifs from those obsessions popping up all over the collection—regal charms, ironic crests, and loads of leopard print—the Alexa has been given a plum loopy leopard quilted denim makeover. I love looking through the Mulberry archives, but anything can inspire me, from my beautiful son Hudson, films and my fabulous design team to pictures and paintings.

47

See Fifi wear this classic Mackintosh on page 26.

FL. *Your mother was an artist—how did that influence you growing up?*

EH. My mother was such an inspiration! Our house was crammed with books, paintings, and pottery. She was so creative, but more than anything she instilled an amazing work ethic in me. Generally though, I'm a huge fan of all kinds of artistic expression.

FL. *Stella loves her canvas doggy raincoat! Are you thinking of extending your dog-wear range and, if so, would you follow on from your bag line —after the raging success of the Alexa!—and name designs after celebrity pooches?*

EH. We have some gorgeous dog stuff coming for A/W '10. Cashmere coats and Fair Isle doggy sweaters that match the Mulberry girl outfits!

FL. *What is your favorite thing you've ever designed? And why?*

EH. I try not to look back too much when I design, so I don't really have one particular favorite. I love the process of making something new. It's exciting to see your ideas become a reality.

FL. *What is "style" to you?*

EH. I think true style comes from within; it's not about the latest trend or what everyone else is wearing. It's knowing what works for you and having fun with it!

FL. *Oh, just one more question. I want to feel comfortable while lounging around at home but still look good, in case I have a surprise visitor. What shall I wear today?*

EH. How about this from spring 2010?

The epitome of easy chic. I love it!
bunny kisses
fifi lapin
xxx

Fun Fur All

Or, how to cull cool looks from your closet . . .

Marc Jacobs

Wednesday

It's raining cats and dogs outside, so I decided to have a big wardrobe tidy. I pulled everything out and spread clothes, shoes, bags, and scarves all over the floor. I must admit it took a lot longer than I thought it would. Now I'm meant to arrange everything into categories, but quite frankly it is dull, dull, dull. Legendary photographer Cecil Beaton said, "Perhaps the world's second-worst crime is boredom; the first is being a bore." So I've decided to embrace the chaos and throw an impromptu party. The wonderful thing about reorganizing your wardrobe is that it encourages you to combine items you wouldn't normally wear together. I'm thinking frills, feathers, and pom-poms as I plan an outfit that will pay homage to the designers who take playful fashion very seriously . . .

Fifi's TIPS *for Dressing Up, Courtesy of My Dream Guest List*

MAKE AN ENTRANCE

Bianca Jagger arrived at her twenty-seventh birthday party looking gorgeous in a draped drop-shoulder Halston dress, riding a white horse led by a naked man—enough said.

COMMIT TO YOUR LOOK

Chloë Sevigny practically invented quirky vintage. And you have to admire her dedication. When she was young, *Little House on the Prairie* was her favorite show, so she had an extreme calico-print dress phase—and even slept in one of those little nightcaps. If you're going to work a look, work it thoroughly.

DARE TO BARE

In a recent interview with *Rolling Stone*, Lady Gaga explained that she rarely wears trousers because "My grandmother is basically blind, but she can make out the lighter parts, like my skin and hair. She says, 'I can see you, because you have no pants on.'" You may not have a blind grandmother, but parties are the perfect time for showing off a little toned arm, shapely leg, or sunkissed back—and the lighting is often much more flattering than it is in daytime.

BE A CONVERSATION PIECE

Holly Golightly (played by Audrey Hepburn in *Breakfast at Tiffany's*, one of my favorite films) and the little black dress go together like carrots and lettuce, but she also had a wonderful way with interiors. Remember the bathtub with gold feet that she used as a sofa and the way she kept her telephone in a suitcase? Even if your dress is classic, you can have fun subverting expectations in other ways.

PLAN AHEAD

In 1992, Vivienne Westwood was deservedly awarded an OBE by the Queen of England. At the ceremony, Westwood was captured by a photographer pantyless in the courtyard of Buckingham Palace. She later said, "I wished to show off my outfit by twirling the skirt. It did not occur to me that, as the photographers were practically on their knees, the result would be more glamorous than I expected." A lesson for us all there!

PROM QUEEN Betsey Johnson's 2007 show was an absolute smorgasbord of party dresses. Inspired by the girl whose "life is just a prom," it featured all the decades: huge '50s crinolines, '60s baby-dolls, and '70s psychedelic print minidresses. My particular gown is pure '80s chic (did the specs give it away?), and I feel like a rainbow-iced cupcake. In fact, it makes me so happy I want to do one of Betsey's signature end-of-show catwalk cartwheels!

Yummy!

Betsey Johnson

Sonia Rykiel

D&G

TEXTURE SHOW Add visual interest and show you have fashion flair by adding some texture to your gown.

Sonia Rykiel. Baby blue is not necessarily a color I would go for in a party dress; it implies far too much innocence! However, in the hands of knitwear legend Sonia Rykiel, who can even make sweaters sexy, this gorgeous silk chiffon number becomes a waterfall of fun. The shape is great for hiding any lumps and bumps, although the platforms are a definite must to create a long and lean silhouette.

D&G. The benefit of this cushioned dress is that if I feel tired at any point in the evening I can just curl up in a corner and have forty winks. No seriously, I really love this little dress. Even with the padding, it is so cleverly constructed it still absolutely flatters, and what a great example of how to match up your accessories; just look at that curtain tassel belt!

Swap the laces in your brogues for pretty ribbon.

GOLD STARS Now that I have everything out of the wardrobe, I have started discovering pieces I forgot I even owned. I can't fathom why, as some of these dresses can only be described as memorable and would surely help make my entrance unforgettable. Just thinking back to Bianca's entrance, I wonder if Stella could stand in for a horse?

Monique Lhuillier. Well, I was looking for fun, and I certainly found it in this piece. This gorgeous little number reminds me of a high-wire artist I used to know; we fell out over a boy. He was seduced by her natural ability to perform somersaults bareback on a horse as it cantered around the ring. Apparently my natural ability to wear a ruffle was no competition.

Monique Lhuillier

GET SHORTY Forget being serious; parties are all about having fun. Go for something short and set those legs free on the dance floor. Fifi Lapin: licence to flirt!

Remember, high neckline + sleeves = ability to carry off super-short skirt.

A tiny waist is a must with a voluminous skirt.

This textural detailing adds an expensive-looking touch.

Bunny ears are so de rigueur and super-handy if you're not lucky enough to be able to wear them au naturel like moi!

Long gloves add a touch of Hollywood glamor.

A high waistline gives the illusion of a longer leg.

Wearing a dark color on your bottom half is ultra slimming.

This is great for hiding a big bum like mine.

Match up your accessories.

Prada

Erin Fetherston

Louis Vuitton

Rainbow Rabbit

Or, how to use color for serious impact . . .

I'm planning a splash of colorful eye makeup this evening (that is if I can decide on an outfit!). Colored makeup can be a daunting prospect if you're usually a natural beauty, but it's a super-fun way of getting a fresh new look and will show off your playful side. Eye makeup is available in a veritable buffet of colors in myriad textures, so the options really are endless. Just let your imagination run wild and see what you come up with!

Fifi's TIPS *for Color Confidence*

⭐ *When a bold color takes center stage, the rest of your makeup should be clean and simple. Same goes for the old rule: lips* or *eyes. We don't want to look like a drag queen now do we?*

⭐ *With any eye makeup look, don't neglect those eyebrows. After neatening them with the help of some tweezers, try using an eyebrow pencil. It's amazing the way a defined pair of brows can lift the face. Choose an eyebrow pencil that is closest in color to your hair and apply using short strokes following the line of the hair growth.*

★ *If you're feeling more confident, choose shades on opposite sides of the color wheel to find complementary colors. Try a yellow shadow with a line of klein blue, shocking pink next to apple green, or turquoise with orange.*

★ *Go for a good-quality brand that will have better staying power.*

★ *Don't be too heavy-handed with your chosen shade, or creasing may occur.*

★ *Start off by patting on some good-quality eye base. It's extra important your makeup doesn't migrate when color is concerned.*

★ *If you want to make a subtle statement, try combining a neutral color with your chosen bright.*

★ *If you're feeling a bit nervous but still want to experiment, try adding a colored mascara on the tips of your lashes after an undercoat of black. Or how about a simple line of colored eyeliner along your top lash line?*

★ *Remember, it's much easier to start slow and build to the full color that you desire. It's no fun breaking out the makeup remover and having to start all over again.*

Fifi's CARROT Cupcakes

FOR THE CAKES

2 EGGS
⅝ CUP SUNFLOWER OIL
¾ CUP SOFT BROWN SUGAR
1¾ CUPS SELF-RISING FLOUR
2 MEDIUM CARROTS, COARSELY GRATED
3 TEASPOONS MIXED SPICE
1 TEASPOON VANILLA EXTRACT
FINELY GRATED ZEST OF 1 ORANGE

1. Preheat the oven to 350° Fahrenheit and put 18 to 20 cupcake liners in muffin tins.

2. Beat the eggs, oil, and brown sugar in a large bowl with an electric mixer for about 3 minutes until light and fluffy.

3. Sift the flour into the bowl and, using a large metal spoon, gently fold with the grated carrots, mixed spice, vanilla, and orange zest, until all the ingredients are combined.

4. Divide the mixture between the cupcake liners and bake for 18 to 20 minutes until well risen and golden brown. Place on a cooling rack.

FOR THE FROSTING

9 OUNCES CREAM CHEESE
½ CUP CONFECTIONERS' SUGAR

Beat together the cream cheese and sugar until smooth. It's a good idea to chill the icing in the fridge while the cakes cool completely. I like to use a piping bag to ice the cakes Magnolia Bakery–style, but if you haven't got one, you can simply smooth it over with a flat knife.

CARROT SPRINKLES
½ cup sugar
¼ cup water
2 grated carrots

1. Put the sugar and water in a small pan and bring to a boil, stirring continuously with a wooden spoon.
2. Add the carrots and reduce the heat. Continue cooking for about 10 minutes.
3. Remove from the heat and let sit for about 5 minutes.
4. Take out the carrot with a slotted spoon, leaving it to cool on a wire rack.
5. When the carrot is completely cool, chop and break up into sprinkles.
6. Sprinkle over your delicious iced cupcakes.

I am so indecisive. I just couldn't decide what to wear. . . . Time to call in an expert!

Barbara Hulanicki

AN ART DECO PALACE OF APRICOT MARBLE AND LEOPARD-SKIN WALLS. FIVE FLOORS OF DECADENT FASHION HEAVEN AND THE LIKELIHOOD OF BUMPING INTO MARIANNE FAITHFULL OR TWIGGY ON YOUR WAY OUT OF THE CHANGING ROOM. IT COULD ONLY BE BIBA, THE LEGENDARY EMPORIUM THAT PRACTICALLY INVENTED MAIN STREET FASHION. THOUGH THE FAMOUS GLOSSY BLACK DOORS CLOSED IN 1976, BARBARA HULANICKI HAS REMAINED A SEMINAL DESIGNER. NEXT TIME YOU FIND YOURSELF IN THE BAHAMAS, I DO RECOMMEND TAKING A SUITE AT THE PINK SANDS OR THE CORAL SANDS—BOTH DESIGNED BY HULANICKI.

FL. How would you describe the girl who chooses to wear Biba?

BH. Well, the girls would come in rather frumpy—there was so little choice around then— the only colors available were a horrible dead red, a horrible royal blue, and a horrible pinky beige. But it was like dressing dolls. British women have the longest legs in the world and everyone was very, very skinny—there wasn't much interest in food then, and not much meat around at all. When the first Wimpy opened, it was really exciting; we used to spend all our profits taking the shop girls there on a Friday night.

FL. Do you still have any of your original clothes?

BH. I don't have anything. I think there are some drawings somewhere in somebody's attic. After Biba finished, my husband and I went to Brazil. I was holding on to various pieces and patterns like a security blanket until one day he said I'd never move on until we got rid of them. So we packed everything up into a truck, took it to a *favela* (slum), and dumped it all. Just as we were driving away, I looked back to see people picking through the piles, looking at the label and discarding the clothes. It was quite a revelation.

FL. *When you started designing, you couldn't buy black—the horror, the horror! Are there certain colors you gravitate toward?*

BH. Black was limited to couture. I still love wearing black but living in Miami with the sunshine, you tend to go much brighter. Last time I was in London, I noticed the wisteria, and it seemed like the whole city was dressed in lilac and rose-pink; it was beautiful. Blue is always good in England, particularly good with blue eyes; yellows and oranges work much better in America. But it's pink that has been through the biggest transformation. It used to be such a taboo color. You could do orchid-pink, but you'd never have it in a room. And now I see it everywhere—I blame Barbie.

FL. *You once said that anything rebellious is interesting. What's the most rebellious thing you've ever done?*

BH. Rebel levels change—there's not very much to rebel against now. I hate to think what the worst thing I did was. My mother thought there was no hope for me—she was terribly worried—she thought I was very lucky to find someone who would marry me at twenty-four. And working! Most girls didn't have careers—she came to the shop, once at the beginning and once at the end. She thought there was something dreadful going on.

FL. *Yoko Ono once borrowed some clothes from Biba—only to cut the arms off on television for an art piece. What are your top tips for customization?*

BH. I'd say a lack of fear. Watching people create their own looks was the fun of Biba. The shop was full of separates, and certainly at the beginning we didn't even have price tags—everyone knew that everything was easily affordable, which encouraged people to mix things up imaginatively. None of our shop assistants offered advice or recommendations—that seemed like a very old-fashioned thing to do. We gave the girls the space to create their own looks and inspire each other. Lots of women used to come in and do themselves up on their way to work; they used the shop like a big dressing room. The challenge was to make sure they didn't steal the stock.

FL. What do you think was the golden age of women's fashion?

BH. I was always told by my mother and aunt how wonderful the '20s were and what a shame it was that I missed them, but you knew perfectly well that it wasn't that great. And now you hear the same thing said about the '60s—although I do still love the leopard-skin coat I designed for Twiggy. I think we all like to remember our youth as a golden period. Things become much more interesting when you start looking back— and you can let your imagination fill in the gaps.

FL. You've designed many fabulous looking hotels, particularly in Miami. Do you work in a very different way when you're designing properties rather than clothes?

BH. Oh yes, hotels take a lot longer—and buildings aren't as easy to correct as a seam on a dress! If you're lucky, you can design as you go along, but people tend to like everything planned beforehand, so you have to pray that your imagination was on the right track. It's very upsetting to see the way people ruin hotels! Managers always want to put horrible little things all over the place. I've been into bedrooms after we've spent an exhausting amount of time getting things ready, and it makes me want to cry. You give people closets and they never put anything away . . .

FL. I'm throwing a party, so I need to set the tone for a wild night. What shall I wear today?

BH. I think you should wear something very simple and black, but you should work on your tail. Maybe a hairnet on it, scattered with diamonds. The ears should comple- ment the tail—a little net over the ears with a skull cap.

Now I really can't wait to party!
bunny kisses
fifi lapin
xxx

THURSDAY
Fashion Forward

Or, how to wear the latest must-have outfit . . .

Louise Gray

Thursday

Jean Cocteau once professed, "Art produces ugly things which frequently become more beautiful with time. Fashion, on the other hand, produces beautiful things which always become ugly with time." Frankly, I'd expect more sense from a French poet. Anyway my point is that art and fashion have gone paw in glove since, well, forever. The PR for art's new wunderkind is desperate for me to come and see said wunderkind's new show. Apparently few others do the head-cocked-to-one-side look so well and none have such a nuanced "hmmmm" as I do. So I need to be looking my most interesting and original. Time for me to check out our most outré designers.

Fifi's TIPS *for Spotting the Latest Talent...*

READ ALL THE LATEST MAGAZINES

Cover the big players like *Vogue* and *Harper's* but also check out quirky independent publications too; *Lula* and *Pop* are my current faves. Look for any tip-offs about new designers. The more you know about the great big wonderful world of fashion, the more your instincts can be trusted.

PEOPLE-WATCH

A lot of trends come from the street. Spend time hanging out in the most fashionable parts of the fashion capitals—Marais in Paris, Harajuku in Tokyo, Shoreditch in London, Williamsburg in New York—and see if you can spot what's going to be hot. If you can't travel as far and wide as me, check out the best street-style blogs—The Sartorialist, Jak & Jil, and Yvan Rodic are my daily reads.

ALWAYS BE ON THE LOOKOUT FOR THE NEW

Legendary stylist Isabella Blow is famous for having bought Alexander McQueen's entire Saint Martins collection, and Mrs. B (otherwise known as Joan Burstein) of renowned London boutique Browns bought all of John Galliano's graduate collection, kick-starting two very fabulous careers. That's what I call serious talent spotting!

DON'T BE A FASHION VICTIM

Don't wear it if you don't like it—no matter how on-trend it's supposed to be. You need to ooze confidence if you want to be seen as style savvy. When I think about some of the fashion faux pas I have made in my short life, maybe Cocteau had a point.

CLASSIC CATCH "Preen" means to dress or groom oneself with elaborate care, and you can't help strutting just a little bit when you put on one of Justin Thornton and Thea Bregazzi's rock-and-roll concoctions. I remember cooing at their very first collection, which was sold from a tiny boutique on the Portobello Road. They started out with a dishevelled vintage look; old keys adorned dresses, and corsets were made out of recycled hair. A decade on and they're all grown up, consistently wowing the New York catwalks with their chic, progressive style.

Preened to perfection!

Preen

Balenciaga

Viktor & Rolf

Commes des Garçons

SHOW OFF Am I getting ahead of myself? Could I be lucky enough to find the designer of the moment twice? Perhaps I should go for some of the more established style mavericks—just to be on the safe side . . .

Balenciaga. Nicolas Ghesquière is the one to watch when it comes to serious cool. In 1997, at the age of just twenty-five, he was entrusted with the role of head designer at one of the most respected fashion houses in the whole of France. This classic dress from 2007 has always been a favorite. The halter-neck shape is über-flattering, and the mixture of colors and textures will show off my creative tendencies.

Viktor & Rolf. Not many people can claim they have launched their own haute couture fashion house, and these guys really know how to make a catwalk statement. One of my all-time favorite shows of theirs was titled "Russian Doll." A single model was positioned on a revolving platform and dressed by the designers in nine garments, one on top of the other. In this ensemble, I'm guaranteed to turn heads, and if at any point in the evening I feel like I'm not getting enough attention, I could always break out a short concerto on my violin.

Commes des Garçons. Though I am content with having one set of unbelievably attractive long ears, I could go for another set à la conceptual legend Rei Kawakubo's pair. It would make a suitably fitting addition to this lilac "double" dress. It's so conceptual that I may get mistaken for one of the exhibits. Darlings! What fun!

BACK TO THE FUTURE I really should trust my instincts; after all, I'm rarely ever wrong about anything at all. So let's forget the classic for now; it's back to the future. The young and talented are always on the lookout for the new, so it's no surprise they often go all sci-fi and revolutionary on us. If I can embrace their vision, I'm sure to be ahead of the fashion pack.

Louise Goldin. I'm enjoying this robotic French maid look, probably because (thanks to Mrs. Fluffy) cleaning is a real novelty for me. And ever since Madonna donned Jean Paul Gaultier's version, I've always had a soft spot for the conical bra.

Louise Goldin

QUIRKY KOOK Being a wallflower never got anyone noticed, so dare to be different. At the very least, your outfit will be a conversation starter.

If you've got it, flaunt it!

Go for a patterned fabric and wear heels to get away from that "just left the gym" look.

You're sure to get a response in a spandex catsuit.

The sculptured shapes and unusual embellishment make it clear that this is no off-the-rack dress.

A beautiful fit is still important, even when going for something a bit more unusual.

Bag-lady chic is all the rage.

Choose plain shoes to balance your statement dress.

Pop on a flower-pot hat—the ribbon tied under the chin is an essential part of this look.

Layer beautiful fabrics in matching tones.

Danielle Scutt

David Koma

Charles Anastase

Get Ahead

Or, how to make your own style statement . . .

If all this creativity is giving you itchy fingers, I have a solution. Crafts are all the rage at the moment, and you may be surprised to know that even I have been known to turn my paw to needle and thread—well if it's in fashion, how can I refuse? One of my girlfriends holds a weekly craft night; last week we made bandos. Mine was so nice I wore it home.

Bandos are elasticated hairbands that can be worn plain across the forehead, "hippie-style," or with detailing at the side, "flapper-style." We're going to have a go at making the flapper style . . .

Start with a basic hairband. You can buy large fabric-covered elastic hairbands, or you can make your own. To make your own, take approximately 16 inches of ½-inch-wide colored or black flat elastic and sew the ends together to make a circle.

Choose what you are going to decorate your bando with. You can raid your nearest craft store for ready-made flowers and appliqué patches or, for something more unique, try your favorite flea market. You can often find exquisite pieces of embroidery and beadwork for bargain prices. Now, depending on your crafting skills, simply sew, staple, or glue on your decoration over the join mark on your hairband.

If simply sewing a piece of elastic together and sticking on a flower is not quenching your craft thirst, then try making your own decoration. Here are two simple ideas . . .

1. *Take a short length of wide ribbon and sew the ends together to make a circle. Lay the ribbon flat with the join in the center.*
Take a smaller width of ribbon in the same color and wrap it around the center of your wider ribbon a few times to make a bow.
Now take a pretty brooch and attach it to the center of your bow.
Voilà!

2. *Take a length of patterned fabric approximately 24 by 3 inches in size. Cut one of the long sides into large scallops.*
Sew a running stitch along the straight edge. Knot at one end and pull tight to gather the fabric into a flower shape. Tie the excess threads together.
Sew a cute button onto the center of the flower.
Voilà!

HOW TO WEAR YOUR BANDO

If you decide to wear your hair down, use a couple of bobby pins to hold the bando in place. A loose, tousled style looks best with this way of wearing.
or
If you like to wear your hair up, try this chic alternative to the ponytail. Put the bando around your neck, keeping in mind where you want the decoration to be. Lift the front onto your forehead (over the top of your bangs if you have them) while letting the back of the band rise up under your hair. Take the ends of your tresses as if you are making a ponytail, tuck them under the elastic, and adjust until you have formed a cute cropped look. Curly or wavy hair with more texture works brilliantly with this style.

Fifi's GREENS ARE GOOD FOR YOU *Detox Drink*

When you've been partying just a little too much, this antioxidant-rich, energy-boosting drink will make you feel as if you're trying to be good.

2 LARGE ORGANIC CARROTS *(a good source of vitamin A; great for skin, hair, and nails)*
2 LARGE ORGANIC TOMATOES *(a diet high in tomatoes can lower your risk of developing some cancers)*
1 STALK ORGANIC CELERY *(full of vitamin C, which helps support the immune system)*
½ ORGANIC CUCUMBER *(a great digestive aid, cucumbers have a cleansing effect on the bowel)*
A HANDFUL OF FRESH ORGANIC SPINACH LEAVES *(a rich source of chlorophyll, which acts as a colon cleanser)*
SMALL BUNCH OF FRESH ORGANIC PARSLEY *(high in enzymes, parsley can help aid digestion)*
A HANDFUL OF ORGANIC LETTUCE LEAVES *(as a general rule, darker green leaves are more nutritious, so ditch the iceberg and reach for the romaine)*

Pop all the ingredients into a juicer or blender, mix well, and serve in a tall glass. Garnish optional.

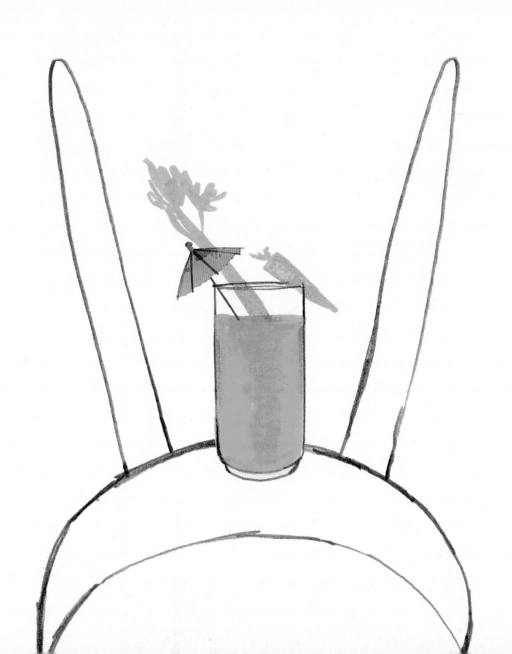

*I am so indecisive.
I just couldn't decide
what to wear. . . . Time
to call in an expert!*

Michael van der Ham

THE CENTRAL SAINT MARTINS GRADUATE, NICKNAMED THE PATCHWORK PRINCE, HAS BEEN TURNING HEADS WITH HIS CREATIONS. MADE BY SEWING TOGETHER SWATCHES OF CONTRASTING FABRICS, HIS DRESSES ARE ECCENTRIC, ELEGANT, AND FLATTERING. AFTER STUDYING FASHION IN HOLLAND, HE WORKED FOR SOPHIA KOKOSALAKI AND ALEXANDER MCQUEEN AND HAD HIS DEBUT SHOW AT LONDON FASHION WEEK IN 2009.

FL. *How would you describe the girl who chooses to wear Michael van der Ham?*

MVDH. Someone who enjoys wearing something quite fun and individual.

FL. *Tell us a little about your label; have you got a defined signature style?*

MVDH. Mismatched, clashing, and real fashion.

FL. What was the first thing you made?

MVDH. When I was sixteen, I made a patchwork mini-skirt. It was badly sewn and had a racy slit.

FL. Your Central Saint Martins MA collection was brilliantly received. What was the inspiration behind it?

MVDH. I saw a look book of some dresses that Andy Warhol designed for an exhibition curated by Diana Vreeland in the '70s. They were created from bits of other dresses by big designers of that era, like Diane von Furstenberg, Halston, Oscar de la Renta, and Valentino. A sleeve from one dress was attached to the front of a different dress. They didn't appeal to me at first, but then I thought the irony of cutting up couture gowns and sewing them back together was really funny. Who would do that? It inspired my graduate collection, but I expanded the source material from the '70s to include shapes from the '20s, '50s, and '60s. And I've continued to play with the idea. I love the element of surprise in putting together clashing fabrics, colors, and cuts.

FL. Your designs take pieces (literally!) from many different decades. If you had to choose one decade to reference, which would it be?

MVDH. I can't choose; I love them all!

FL. Which other young designers are you excited about at the moment?

MVDH. I love London designers Christopher Shannon's reworked luxe sportswear and Mary Katrantzou's signature prints.

FL. Your latest collection was sponsored by Liberty; how did that work out for you?

MVDH. Liberty were kind enough to allow me into their print archives, and I found some beautiful fabrics.

FL. I particularly loved your floor-length navy silk gown with crystal-encrusted beige wool patchwork from the latest collection. Would you like to see your work grace the red carpet?

MVDH. Sure. I'd like to see stars wear my work to red-carpet events, however I don't think it's my priority at the moment. As a new designer just starting out, it can be quite hard getting dresses onto stars.

FL. What can we expect from you next?

MVDH. I'll continue showing at London Fashion Week and grow my international stockists.

FL. I'm going to a private opening tonight and want to make a statement. What shall I wear today?

MVDH. A Liberty fabric-print paneled dress by Michael van der Ham.

Cute and conceptual—brilliant!
bunny kisses
fifi lapin
xxx

24-Carrot-Gold
Glamor

Or, how to set the flashbulbs popping for red-carpet moments . . .

Friday

I am ever so slightly overexcited because, my darlings, I have in my sticky little paw an invitation to the red-carpet event of the year, possibly even the century. All the biggest stars will be making an appearance, so I better be on my toes if I want to get noticed. I'm determined to make an impact and will be flirting outrageously with all the paparazzi!

Fifi's TIPS *for a Dramatic Red-Carpet Look...*

★ Forget separates. A long gown is the only way to go if you're looking for full-on glamor.

★ Make sure your dress fits really well. All of us are guilty of falling for an item on the hanger and fooling ourselves in the changing room. Just remember, after a few hours of wear, it will show all over your face. A pained expression is not a good look.

★ Find a shape and style that suits your figure. See below for more tips. Not all of us are fortunate enough to be born with my knack of carrying off any look.

★ Fabulous or wacky—know the difference. If you go for wacky, have a witty retort at the ready to combat any negative reactions. Remember you are a slave to fashion and you are simply expressing that.

★ Don't undersell yourself. Even simple can be done with impact. Shoulders back, head held high, think confident, think me, me, me.

PETITE Don't drown in fabric. The vertically challenged can still do long, but avoid the puddle effect around your feet. Large details around the neckline and voluminous sleeves are also a big no-no.

BOYISH A long empire-line dress can look fabulous on the less-endowed figure. Reveal a good amount of skin around the neckline for femininity and add detailing around the bust to boost your lack of assets.

HOURGLASS Work it girl! Corseting is great for enhancing your knockout look. If your hips are on the generous side, wear a padded bra to balance you out. Avoid anything with a high neck or no waistline—frumpiness is guaranteed.

FULLER FIGURE Soft fabrics in draped styles can be great for the fuller figure. Make sure you pull in the draping at the waist to accentuate your sexy curves.

NOTICE ME   Prints are a sure-fire way to turn up the volume on your outfit. To avoid being overwhelmed—remember it's you wearing the print, not the print wearing you—choose a fine fabric that will move gracefully, keep the line of the dress clean, and ditch any fussy accessories. Not everybody can pull off an eye-catching color—if you've got skin even nearing orange put it down immediately!—but it's perfect for me with my porcelain complexion. Technicolor shades are instant mood lifters, so if I choose this gown, I know I'll make the paps smile.

*Turn your dress
up to max-imum!*

BCBGMAXAZRIA

Rodarte

D&G

SHAPELY SEDUCTRESS

On second thought, maybe full-on glamor is a bit obvious. Back to the drawing board. As Grandmother Lapin (God rest her paws) always told me, get the silhouette right and the rest will follow. If a dress fits your body beautifully, you will be sure to shine. So I looked through my wardrobe again and thought about myself against a stark black background. Try the same at home.

Rodarte. Oh, the Mulleavy sisters are so clever. Apparently they're inspired by '60s zombie films, but slip on one of their dip-dyed chiffon numbers and you can't help but feel all dreamy and romantic. There's no point wearing this if you've got bingo wings, but all that draping on the skirt means you don't need to skip lunch or wear Spanx.

D&G. Ooooh, this is tempting. One of the best things about being an international style icon is that you can walk down a red carpet in the kind of dress normally reserved for walking down the aisle. Before you think about going the meringue route, work out how you're getting to and from places, and how much sitting down you'll be doing when you're there. This is going to be a squeeze— I'm not entirely sure it will fit in my limo.

Pucci. Does anybody do eye-popping prints better than legendary Italian label Pucci? Putting on one of their dresses puts me in mind of their other iconic fans like Jackie O and Elizabeth Taylor—sigh. And the asymmetric neckline allows me to show a little fur and avoid looking too swamped in magic-eye patterns.

Pucci

Marchesa

Marchesa. Another gorgeous little asymmetric number. This shape does seem to lend itself so well to printed fabrics. This beautiful Marchesa gown features a more subtle print with the main impact coming from the crisscross bands of black. The cutaway sections balance out the cute bow and transform it from super-sweet to ever so sexy.

ACCESSORIZE One of the things that sets me apart in the style stakes is my willingness to go the extra mile. Do not relax simply because you've found the right dress. Accessorizing is an art— treat it with the respect it deserves and you will be rewarded. Not too little, not too much. I've been known to wear the same LBD on more than one occasion, and I swear, thanks to a clever use of jewels, belts, clutches, and shoes, no one knew! Amazing.

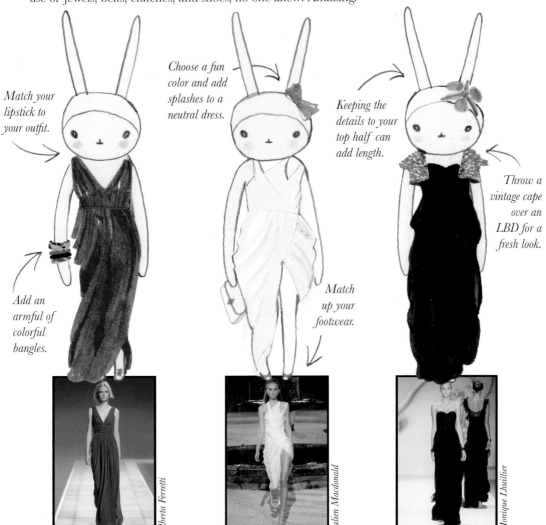

Match your lipstick to your outfit.

Choose a fun color and add splashes to a neutral dress.

Keeping the details to your top half can add length.

Throw a vintage cape over an LBD for a fresh look.

Add an armful of colorful bangles.

Match up your footwear.

Alberta Ferretti

Julien Macdonald

Monique Lhuillier

95

Ravishing Rabbit

Or, how to create the perfect vintage starlet look...

The vintage look is so stylish. So why stop at your outfit when you can get makeup tips from the gals who made the silver screen so iconic? The ultra-feminine, ultra-flattering cat's eye suits all eye shapes, so it's a real favorite of mine. It does take a bit of practice, but once you've perfected it, you won't be able to put down that liquid liner! Sometimes I like to dress my eyes like this in the daytime with a simple white tee, skinny jeans, and a Hermès headscarf for a rockabilly-inspired look. You can even break the cardinal rule of lips or eyes and add a super-bold lipstick. Try a matte shade for a modern take on classic red.

1. *Prepare your eye. Dab some primer over your entire lid. This will stop all your hard work from sliding off halfway through the evening. Apply your eyeshadow as usual if you want a smokier look.*

2. *Take your liquid eyeliner and start by drawing a fine line along the lash line only. The key is to get that line as close as possible to your lash line. Try tilting your head up and look down at the mirror; your lid should close just enough while still allowing you to see.*

3. *Once your line is perfect, carefully extend it upward into a subtle flick using your lower eye line as a guide. Repeat with the other eye.*

4. *Look into the mirror with a relaxed face. That means no raised eyebrows (if you have them)! Check the flicked ends are even.*

5. *Neaten the flicks and thicken the outer ends of the liner for a more winged shape.*

6. *Add your favorite mascara. Now practice letting your eyes drift coyly downward, so that others may admire that steady line and, as you lift your long lashes, say, "Who, me?" in a dreamy voice. I did this the night I first met Sonny Hare—he's never forgotten it.*

EXTRA TIPS...

⭐ Practice makes perfect, so try this a few times well in advance of your event.

⭐ Rest your elbow on something stable for a steady paw.

⭐ If there's too much liquid liner on your brush, just wipe a bit of the excess onto the back of your paw—remember, less is more.

⭐ You don't have to draw everything all in one go. If you prefer to make short strokes, that's fine; just take it steady.

⭐ Keep Q-tips and eye-makeup remover handy for little touch-ups.

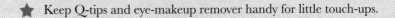

Fifi's TIPS *for How to Pose in Front of the Camera...*

★ To appear slimmer in a full-length shot, turn your body partially sideways to the camera, with one foot in front of the other. Point your toe to the camera and place your weight on your back foot. Now gently rotate your shoulders toward the front.

★ If you're on the curvy side, try putting a hand on one hip with your elbow straight out and lean your upper body away from the arm to get some space between the two. This will give you more shape and definition at the waist

★ If the camera is at eye level or below, lower your chin very slightly.

★ Try not to be shot from below, this will foreshorten you and make you look wider—eek!

★ Harsh lighting can create ugly shadows, so try to avoid direct sunlight.

★ Set your gaze beyond the camera. Focus on something in the distance for a more natural look.

★ Smiling with your teeth will often give the most genuine results. If you're looking for a more serious expression, try gently trapping your tongue between your teeth and opening your mouth a little à la Kate Moss.

★ Forget saying "cheese." The Olsen twins are said to whisper the word "prune" for a more seductive pout.

★ Relax! Holding your breath will only make you appear uptight and awkward, so remember to breathe.

> *I am so indecisive.
> I just couldn't decide
> what to wear. . . . Time
> to call in an expert!*

Erdem

OH, HOW I MARVEL OVER ERDEM'S CREATIONS. EACH DESIGN IS BLESSED WITH AN AMAZING SENSE OF CRAFTSMANSHIP; WHETHER INTRICATELY EMBROIDERED, LACE ADORNED, OR APPLIQUÉD WITHIN AN INCH OF ITS LIFE, IT IS ALWAYS BEAUTIFUL. HE IS ALSO FAMOUS FOR HIS PRINTS, OFTEN MODERN AND PHOTOGRAPHIC IN ESSENCE YET ALWAYS LOOKING BACK TO A TIME OF ROMANTICISM—SWOON! IF ANYONE KNOWS HOW TO DRESS A GIRL, IT'S HIM; AND IF YOU DON'T BELIEVE ME, JUST ASK HOLLYWOOD STARLETS KEIRA KNIGHTLEY, GWYNETH PALTROW, AND THANDIE NEWTON, WHO HAVE ALL WALKED THE RED CARPET IN HIS GORGEOUS GOWNS. SO HOW DOES HE KNOW WHAT WOMEN REALLY WANT—BE THEY A LEADING LADY OR A FIRST LADY? (YES, MICHELLE OBAMA IS ALSO A FAN.) MAYBE IT'S HAVING A TWIN SISTER? MAYBE IT'S HAVING GROWN UP WATCHING THE MERCHANT IVORY FILMS HIS ANGLOPHILE MOTHER LOVED? OR MAYBE IT'S JUST KNOWING THAT DEEP DOWN EVERY GIRL LONGS TO BE FEMININE WITHOUT BEING TOO SWEET?

FL. How would you describe the girl who chooses to wear Erdem?

E. The Erdem wearer marches to her own drum. She doesn't pay attention to seasons or trends; she just wears what she wants and in a unique manner. She has an effortless style and puts things together with a free spirit.

FL. The reason I adore your collections is your unique use of color, pattern, and texture. Can you explain a little how your creative process happens?

E. I'm inspired by anything and everything: photographs, paintings, dance, music, my friends. My creative process is accidental. It's a lot of playing around and experimenting. I usually start with one thing and it morphs into another and that happens a few times until it feels right.

FL. Your shows are the hot ticket of London Fashion Week. Does the deadline of having to show a collection twice a year help or hinder your creative process?

E. The show deadline helps to a certain extent because you work toward a goal. Often stress can be a catalyst for creativity.

FL. Do you draw as part of your creative process?

E. Yes, I do draw. It is very much a part of my creative process. Here are two illustrations from spring 2010.

FL. Gorgeous! I absolutely love the collage element. Fashionistas such as myself look to young designers for the next big thing. How important is it to you to create something unique?

E. It's the backbone of what I do. I like the concept of creating something special and knowing that the wearer is the only person in the world that has that unique dress.

FL. *It's clear I'm obsessed with fashion, but tell me about your latest obsession.*

E. I'm very much a fan of Ryan McGinley's new photographic series, Moonmilk, which has been collected into a book. There's something so pagan and colorful about his pictures.

FL. *Have you got any advice for any budding fashion designers out there?*

E. Perseverance is key. There will be a lot of people who tell you that you can't do it, but if you know what you're doing, carry on. And know who your customer is. You need to understand what you are making and who will wear it.

FL. *What is "style" to you?*

E. Style is an innate, instinctual ability to be effortlessly individual in whatever you do.

FL. *Oh, just one last question. I'm going to the movie premiere of the year. What shall I wear today?*

E. Because you are a bunny, I think you should wear something with bold color; you want something that stands out from the red of the carpet. So I've picked this printed-silk bias-cut dress with contrasting navy ruffle detail. It definitely shows off your feminine side in a sophisticated way. Of course, we would make a little adjustment for your bunny tail.

It's truly stunning. Thank you!
bunny kisses
fifi lapin
xxx

SATURDAY
Paris, J'Adore

Or, how to dress for the most fashionably perfect date . . .

Miu Miu

Saturday

Ooh la la! My beau, the darling Sonny Hare, is whisking me off to Paris, the city of love, for a surprise date. He called me very, very early this morning, and I was a bit grumpy with him, to be honest. A bunny needs her beauty sleep after all! But I have forgiven him as the thought of tripping down the Champs-Élysées in the spring sunshine is filling my heart with joy. As I'm sure I don't need to remind you, Paris is the absolute capital of sophisticated style, something to keep foremost in my mind while I'm picking an outfit. And as this also happens to be a date, I need to look absolutely darling. I do relish a challenge—after all, that's what keeps my style looking fresh and new—but I only have an hour to get ready, so I'd better make it snappy . . .

Fifi's TIPS *for a Successful Date . . .*

★ I can't say it enough: preparation, preparation, preparation! Being a natural furball, I don't have any issues with unwanted hair, but for you gals, I suggest waxing within an inch of your life. Well-manicured nails are a must and having a freshly brushed set of pearly whites goes without saying.

★ Spray only a light spritz of your signature fragrance. Too much and he'll be reminded of his lavender-scented granny. Same goes for makeup—he'll avoid going in for the kiss if he thinks he's going to come away wearing more than you.

★ Choose an outfit that makes you feel confident. If you think you look gorgeous, he'll have no option but to agree. Soft, natural fibers will feel good against your skin—and his.

★ Whatever you're wearing, make sure it fits. It sounds obvious, but if your clothes have mysteriously shrunk, you'll spend all day yanking and pulling and fidgeting. This will make it quite impossible to navigate the Métro with the appropriate amount of Parisian élan.

★ Avoid the temptation to totter out in your brand-new skyscraper heels. Always wear shoes that you've broken in, at least a bit. And always carry Band-Aids, just in case of an unforeseen blister.

★ Carry a practical bag. You don't want to be lugging around the kind that doubles as a suitcase, but you need one capacious enough to take care of the essentials. A hand-kerchief is invaluable for wiping up whatever—though only a fool would go for spaghetti vongole on a date. I recommend a small bottle opener in case you fancy wine alfresco. And pack a safety pin. It's not as cumbersome as a Swiss Army knife but is almost as multipurpose. And never, ever leave home without a lipstick.

PRETTY CHIC Oh, to live in Paris! Just imagine popping down to the local *boulangerie* on a sunny morning, wearing a romantic flower-print dress and chic little shoes topped off with perfectly cute bows. As a long-time fan of Cynthia's designs, I would say the typical Cynthia girl is the epitome of carefree cool, and this dress from the spring 2010 collection proved that looking pretty can still look young and fresh.

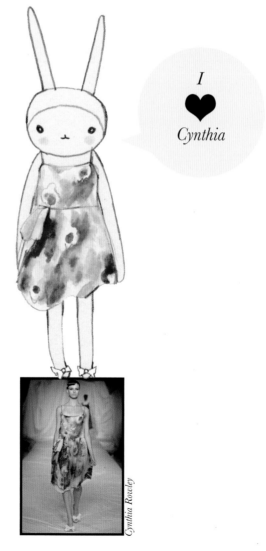

I ♥ Cynthia

Cynthia Rowley

Alberta Ferretti

Fendi

PRETTY PERFECT I thought I had cracked it on my very first search, but then I spotted these little beauties. Surely the theme of the day should be pretty. After all, the point of the outfit is to make me look utterly irresistible.

Alberta Ferretti. The queen of "ultra-feminine, guaranteed to make you feel gorgeous" dresses does it again with this little chiffon number. The pinstripes and sensible belt stop the look from being too sweet, and I love the idea of wearing practical brogues. Not only do they look super-cute, they are also super-comfy for traipsing around the *arrondissements*.

Fendi. Well, I know I can trust Fendi when it comes to French dressing. They even revived the "it" bag phenomenon with their appropriately named "Baguette" bag. It's true—wherever you are in Paris, there will always be someone carrying a French stick within eyeshot. The "dream beach" colors of this outfit are to die for. Creamy white, palest sea green, and a splash of coral. How can Sonny fail to be romantic while gazing at me wearing this?

*E*mbrace opaque tights to take your spring clothes into fall.

LEGGY LADY Dresses and skirts always spring to mind when I think about dressing for romance, but then I thought, why not go for something a bit different? Trousers don't have to be confined to the sensible side of your wardrobe. From the straight and skinny to the super-tight, balloon, and harem, the runway is awash with styles. Just choose a pretty color or team with cutesy detailing, and you'll look effortlessly chic.

Eley Kishimoto. I'll forgive this outfit for not featuring one of Eley Kishimoto's famous lust-worthy prints because it's just darling. The gently shaped harem trousers are great for all shapes and sizes and as a bonus come in a soft silk that adds a touch of class. The dickie bow and faux button front are a sweet touch, too.

Viktor & Rolf

Eley Kishimoto

Viktor & Rolf. The avant-garde design duo certainly know how to vamp up the sex appeal of trousers. I may look as if I just stepped out of a vintage boudoir, but I assure you, underwear as outerwear is a trend that has been revisited on the catwalk more times than I've had carrot-based dinners. I suggest you follow V & R's lead and rock it up a bit by including some black detailing with your pastel lace.

SHORT AND SWEET Plug in the Power Plate and roll out the yoga mat; it's time to tone up those legs, ladies. If you're feeling daring, short hems, be they on dresses, skirts, shorts, or culottes, are a winner in the sexy style stakes. If you've been hiding your limbs away from the light of day, treat them to a toning massage with a gentle exfoliater, add some self-tanner, and finish off with a dusting of shimmer powder.

Chunky tribal jewelry against graphic stripes makes an unusual yet pleasing combination.

Statement shoulders balance out the puffball shape of the miniskirt.

This pretty dress has just the right amount of sex appeal to stop me from looking too cutesy.

Balance out a busy print with a block of neutral color.

The barely-there effect of the spaghetti straps will be lost if your bra straps are on show. Invest in a good-quality strapless bra.

A flirty A-line skirt is great for skimming over more generous proportions.

Wear sequins in the day— just keep them bright.

Louis Vuitton

Gucci

Tibi

113

Bewitching Bunny

Or, how to do pretty perfect makeup . . .

As you know, I'm in a serious hurry this morning. I still haven't chosen what to wear today, so quite frankly I haven't got the time or the patience for sitting on my bum in front of the mirror. If you need to get made up in a flash (or are just plain lazy), all you need are a few key products and a few precious minutes.

1. I am a big fan of mineral powders because they not only give great natural coverage but also, over time, can even improve the health and condition of your skin. You need to start off by applying a light moisturizer, especially if your skin is dry. Let it properly sink in before applying your base. You can use this time for grabbing some breakfast—that's a carrot and raisin muffin for me.

2. I recommend buying a really good-quality, large, dense-bristled brush. Swirl the head of the brush around the pot to pick up the mineral powder and then tap off the excess. You only need a light dusting. Brush onto your face using a gentle circular motion. Remember to blend into your neck to avoid creating a mask effect.

3. Sweep a light-reflecting product (I can't live without my YSL Touche Èclat) under your eyes and blend into the skin. If you have any other irritating little shadows, perhaps at the side of the nose or the corners of the mouth, you can apply some there, too—but remember less is more!

4. Apply a concealer for spots only if really necessary (the powder may be enough coverage). First use a small brush, then for a natural finish, blend by patting it into the skin with your finger.

5. Grab a metal eyelash curler and stick it under the hairdryer for a few seconds (make sure it doesn't get too hot! Test it on your hand before your eyelashes). This will help set the curl and make it last all day. Open the curler and clamp the lashes near the roots. Hold for 10 to 30 seconds. Repeat on the other eye.

6. Apply two coats of black mascara. Start at the outside of the eye and work inward. This way the longer lashes at the outer corner of the eye are covered first—when the most mascara is available on the brush. Wiggle the wand through the lashes from base to tip for fullness and length.

7. Use a clear mascara to neaten and set the eyebrows.

8. Add a lightly colored gloss to lips to make them soft and kissable! Pop this in your handbag for touch-ups later.

9. Finally, add the signature Fifi Lapin pink cheeks. Smile, and using a large powder brush, sweep a pretty pink or peach blush onto the apples of your cheeks, blending upward and away with short up-and-down strokes.

Paris Je T'aime

UNION POSTALE UNIVERELLE
CARTE POSTALE
Postcard   Postkarte

Partie réservée à la correspondance

dresse du destinataire

Dear Stella,

Paris j'adore!
We went right to the top of the
'Tour Eiffel'. The tourists looked
so tiny, like little ants. I've
eaten four macaroons. I'll bring
you back a pink one.
au revoir!

bunny kisses
fifi
xxx

Stella c/o Mrs Fluffy

The Burrow

Notting Hill

London UK

> *I am so indecisive.
> I just couldn't decide
> what to wear. . . . Time
> to call in an expert!*

Anna Sui

AFTER LEAVING THE FAMOUS PARSONS NEW SCHOOL FOR DESIGN IN NEW YORK, ANNA SUI BEGAN DESIGNING CLOTHING OUT OF HER APARTMENT. ENCOURAGED BY HER FRIENDS, WHO JUST HAPPENED TO BE SUPERMODELS EXTRAORDINAIRE NAOMI CAMPBELL AND LINDA EVANGELISTA, SHE LAUNCHED HER FIRST RUNWAY SHOW IN 1991. WHEN SHE OPENED HER FIRST BOUTIQUE IN 1992, WITH ITS LAVENDER WALLS, RED FLOORS, ANTIQUE BLACK FURNITURE, AND DOZENS OF PAPIER-MÂCHÉ DOLLY HEADS—INSPIRED BY HAT FORMS SHE'D FOUND IN FLEA MARKETS—SHE CREATED A LOOK THAT HAS BECOME SYNONYMOUS WITH HER BRAND. NOW THE DOLLY HEAD IS GLOBAL—AND SHE'S ADDED FRAGRANCES, COSMETICS, AND ACCESSORIES TO HER CLOTHING LINE. *TIME* MAGAZINE NAMED HER AS ONE OF THE TOP FIVE FASHION ICONS OF THE DECADE (GULP!). AND IN 2009 SHE RECEIVED THE COUNCIL OF FASHION DESIGNERS OF AMERICA LIFE-TIME ACHIEVEMENT AWARD . . . AND SHE HAS FIVE HUNDRED PAIRS OF SHOES. WOW!

FL. How would you describe the girl who chooses to wear Anna Sui?

AS. There's always a very sweet feminine, girly side . . . a touch of nostalgia. Then there's the trendy side . . . the hipness I try to create by adding a rock-and-roll coolness. There's always that ambiguity . . . the "good girl/bad girl" thing.

FL. *You obviously have a real love for texture and print. How do you develop your ideas?*

AS. Developing fabrics takes more time than anything, so that's definitely where I begin the process. Everything evolves from there. At the same time, I like to develop a theme for the collection. I'm fortunate that everything I'm currently interested in can serve as inspiration (films, exhibitions, music, books, travel, flea markets). I love doing research, learning about something new.

FL. *Your work is quite romantic but with a definite edgy side. Where does this aesthetic come from?*

AS. I think I've always been very consistent. When I started designing, my intention was to dress rock stars and people who went to rock concerts . . . and that's what I still do. Music has always been a major influence on me. The Rolling Stones were always my favorite style icons; I always incorporate elements of their look into my personal wardrobe and into what I design for my collection (pinstriped pants, ruffled shirts, tall boots). I've worked many rock themes into my work: punk, glam, goth, folk, mod, grunge, psychedelia.

FL. *I know that you started off as a stylist for Steven Meisel; do you style your own shows?*

AS. I'm so lucky that many of my closest friends are some of the greatest fashion minds of our age (Steven Meisel, Bill Mullen, Paul Cavaco, among others). Through the years, at different times, these friends have made a habit of stopping by for marathon styling sessions (though now sometimes we do it by e-mail). For us it's like a party, playing dress-up, challenging each other to push the boundaries. These are some of my fondest memories.

FL. *You have an amazing double apartment in Manhattan—one brightly colored and rococo, the other a monochrome retreat. Do you apply the same processes to decorating your apartment as you do to your clothes?*

AS. I suppose it's quite similar ... planning and mixing all the details: wallpapers, upholstery fabrics, lighting fixtures, doorknobs. I have a great interest in interior design. ... My main influences are Elsie de Wolfe, the Amalienburg, Mary Blair, the Peacock Room, Rose Cumming, and Serendipity.

FL. *I am especially envious of your "serendipity closet"—a seemingly ordinary yet beautiful armoire leads into a huge walk-in wardrobe. Is keeping a sense of fun important to you?*

AS. I always love a touch of theatrical whimsy; there's a sense of humor in everything I do.

FL. *It's clear I'm passionate about fashion; tell me about your latest passion.*

AS. I just got back from Syria. I am in love with mother-of-pearl and shell-inlaid furniture.

FL. *What is "style" to you?*

AS. For me, style is about spirit and attitude. It's not about age—my mother wears my designs, and so do my nieces (now that they have grown up enough to fit the clothes). It's about having a little fun, opting for a little glamor, not taking yourself so seriously.

FL. *Oh, just one last question. I'm being whisked off to Paris by my beau for a romantic date. What shall I wear today?*

AS. No. 46 from my fall 2010 fashion show.

I can't wait to wow Sonny!
bunny kisses
fifi lapin
xxx

SUNDAY
Dress to Impress

Or, how to make a serious impact . . .

Sunday

Oops! My gold card seems to have given up the ghost. I popped out this morning for a pint of milk (it's Mrs. Fluffy's day off), and as I headed for the corner store I was inexplicably drawn into the Cartier store. I must have been dazzled by all the lovely sparkly stuff in the window. To cut a long story short, I fell in love with a gigantic spangly cocktail ring, just perfect for something or other. When I went to pay, my card was refused. It was terribly embarrassing. Made even more so because I was still wearing my Chanel PJs and fuzzy bunny slippers. I've called a lunch meeting with Daddy and need to do some serious schmoozing. So, an outfit that suggests I'm a rabbit of substance: confident, in control, and to be trusted absolutely to make sensible decisions.

Fifi's TIPS *for Making a Serious Impact...*

★ The power suit is so last century. The new power dressing comes with authenticity. It means owning your look and being at ease with what you're wearing.

★ Tailoring. Always a good bet, it should strike a balance between clean and strong, feminine and fashionable.

★ The yin and the yang. A masculine look can suggest power and authority but may also suggest you are domineering and lack creativity. Wear a lace neckline under a beautifully tailored jacket, and you have the best of both worlds.

★ There's strength in color. A dress in a solid, bold color creates an instant visual impact, a style force to be reckoned with.

★ Less is often more. Keep lines clean and ditch any fussy elements.

★ A high heel exudes confidence. Just make sure you're well practiced at walking in them. I know from experience that falling flat on your face is not going to impress anyone.

★ Boxy cardigans. Everyone should have one: softer and more approachable than a blazer but often just as smart.

ELECTRIC ECLECTIC Eclectic dressing at its best: Marc's muse appears to have been an Asian Americana-loving '50s-film-star secretary. This has all the ingredients of demure dressing with a twist. I love it! You may never have thought of putting together a slightly squashed straw hat, wayfarer-style glasses, a plaid blouse, and an embellished skirt, but in the hands of an expert (and with the help of a buttoned-up corset belt), it all works perfectly and creates a polished look.

Howdy,
Sweet Cheeks!

Marc Jacobs

Charles Anastase

D&G

CHARACTER CASE

Power dressing isn't an excuse for staid and boring. As you know, I like to express my engaging personality through my outfits, and surprise is often the most effective form of attack!

Charles Anastase. It's back to school to learn the basics of smart style. A suit jacket brings instant togetherness to an outfit, and who says ties are just for the boys? These terrifyingly tall platform heels will ensure I command attention, and if all else fails, I could regress to my childhood and have a hissy fit until Daddy gives in!

D&G. I can just imagine walking down the mall admiring Buckingham Palace wearing this gorgeous little ensemble. Someone is bound to mistake me for someone important in this off-duty royal look. Perhaps I should swap Stella for a corgi? At the very least, this headscarf will protect my newly coiffed earstyle.

SOFT TOUCH Maybe something a little less structured would be better? Smart doesn't have to mean hard; perhaps I could take a softer approach and appeal to his more cuddly side. I'm sure he has one somewhere.

Marc by Marc Jacobs. This all-black ensemble still says sensible, but by using a softer shape and lighter fabrics, it's a whole lot more comfortable. The buttoned-up shirt, pulled-in waist, and hat pulled down over the eyes give a sense that you really mean business.

Marc by Marc Jacobs

3.1 Phillip Lim

3.1 Phillip Lim. Phillip always manages to add an air of cool confidence to his clothes, so I'd be in safe hands in this gorgeous draped dress and boxy jacket. Smart doesn't have to mean gloomy. I love the happy mustard color of the jacket, and the cropped proportions allow the knee-length dress to elongate my ample hip area.

QUICK DRAW After a cup of tea and a slice of carrot cake, I came to my senses and realized that in a situation like this, I need to pull out the big guns. The pencil skirt has been around since the '40s, when iconic fashion genius Christian Dior came up with the sexy shape calling it the "H-line" skirt. It was immediately adopted as the working woman's uniform and remains so. Always strong, yet entirely feminine, it has to be the easiest way to dress for success.

To exaggerate that gorgeous hourglass shape, wear your belt over your jacket.

Think vintage when dressing smart. Women in the '40s really knew how to work that sexy secretary look.

A pretty embroidered blouse softens the hard lines of the skirt.

The pencil line doesn't have to be restricted to skirts—this tailored coat is the ultimate lengthening cover-up.

The flash of skin from a peep-toe shoe elongates the leg.

Add a little sex appeal with ankle-strap platforms.

A monochrome palette is a strong statement and will show you really mean business.

If this outfit doesn't say "Check me out; I deserve a nice fat wardrobe," then I don't know what does!

Diane von Furstenberg

Yves Saint Laurent

Prada

131

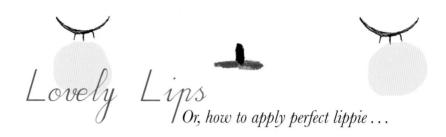

Lovely Lips

Or, how to apply perfect lippie...

The color red is known for its power properties, hence the red power tie for business people and the red carpet for VIPs—like *moi*. Red grabs your attention, sends the pulse racing, and increases your appetite—though that's not so popular in fashion circles. Luscious red-painted lips are a classic beauty look, and for years all the most glamorous gals have been using them to their advantage.

Fifi's TIPS for Finding the Perfect Shade...

⭐ *As a general rule, warm skin tones should opt for a warm, golden-based shade such as a peachy red. Cool skin tones should go for blue- and pink-based tones such as a plummy red. Start by picking out three or four reds that you like and think might work. Apply them to the back of your paw and take a really good look in natural light to see what actually suits your skin. Eliminate any that don't match up before taking the time to test on your face.*

⭐ *Compare the colors to your natural lip color; the closer they are, the more likely it will look fabulous.*

⭐ *Brighter lip colors are more likely to smear, bleed, or feather, so bear this in mind and take precautions when you apply your lipstick.*

⭐ *If you make a mistake and buy the wrong lipstick, don't throw it out right away. You can create a great new lip color by blending lipsticks you don't like.*

HOW TO APPLY . . .

Before you start, make sure your lips are beautifully conditioned. A soft toothbrush is great for this. Slather your lips with petroleum jelly and then just gently brush your lips before rinsing off.

1. Apply a clear, nourishing balm.

2. Apply a soft lip liner over the entire lip. This will stop the lipstick from bleeding and prevents an ugly outlined look as your lipstick wears off.

3. Use a small lip brush to apply a nice creamy lipstick, spreading color from the center of your lips and moving out. Go slow; you can always add more if you need it.

4. Blot your lips gently with a clean tissue and, using a sponge, pat your lips with some colorless, translucent loose powder.

5. Reapply your lipstick.

6. For a full pout, dab the center of your bottom lip with gloss.

STARRING

I am so indecisive. I just couldn't decide what to wear. . . . Time to call in an expert!

Paul Smith

WHO WOULD HAVE THOUGHT AN ACCIDENT COULD LEAD TO BEING KNIGHTED BY THE QUEEN? AT SEVENTEEN, PAUL SMITH'S DREAMS OF BEING A RACING CYCLIST CAME TO AN END. BUT TWO YEARS AFTER BEING EMPLOYED AS THE ERRAND BOY, HE WAS THE MENSWEAR BUYER AT A CLOTHING WAREHOUSE IN NOTTINGHAM. IN 1970 HE OPENED HIS FIRST SHOP, AND NOW THOSE STRIPES, THOSE FLORAL SHIRTS, AND THAT CLASSIC TAILORING WITH A SURPRISING TWIST ARE A GLOBAL EMPIRE! IN 2007 HE BROUGHT HIS TWO GREAT PASSIONS TOGETHER WITH A RANGE OF CLOTHING FOR CYCLISTS, INCLUDING A SUIT WITH EXTENDABLE SLEEVES—THE BOY DONE GOOD!

FL. How would you describe the girl who chooses to wear Paul Smith?

PS. Quite a lot of my customers are creative types, such as singers, graphic designers, and architects, so I like to think of someone that is full of energy and ideas wearing Paul Smith.

FL. You have been long known for your iconic menswear. How do you translate that heritage into your womenswear?

PS. I retain the simplicity of the tailoring, the use of color and mixing patterns, coupled with the surprises—there might be lace around the inside hem of a jacket or a colored buttonhole—that are well known in my clothes for men.

ul Smith's La Tourette
utique in rue de
renelle, Paris, was
iginally a bustling
fé, popular with
riters and artists—
ul made minimal
anges in order to
eserve its history.

See Fifi in this
gorgeous little
number on
page 122.

FL. *How do you start a collection?*

PS. It changes every season, but it might begin with a specific idea that I got from a movie, an art exhibition, or a book, or it can just be working around color and pattern or a combination of both.

FL. *How do you feel when you see people wearing your clothes in the street?*

PS. If they look good, it feels great—if they don't, I hide!

FL. *As well as beautiful clothes, your shops are also treasure troves of interesting objects and curios.*

PS. I am definitely a magpie; you should see my studio! The last thing I found was a great vintage metal biscuit tin which was full of old postage stamps.

FL. *I can't imagine you wearing anything but a suit. Have you ever worn casual clothes?*

PS. I have been wearing suits since I was about eighteen, when I had my first one made. It was mint green, and my second one was dusty pink—I can't imagine wearing colors like that now, but I suppose at eighteen it was OK, very rock and roll! I have always styled suits my own way; it might be with a denim shirt or "the wrong shoes" or a really worn-out belt.

FL. You were knighted by the Queen in 2000 for your services to British fashion. Do you ever use that title to your advantage, and what was it like meeting the Queen?

PS. During a recent visit to Jordan, there was an enormous queue at airport security, which would have meant I'd miss my plane; I used it then and managed to get through the crowds in order to get home! I have always liked the Queen, so it was a pleasure to meet her. I also liked her mum, whom I was lucky enough to meet once.

FL. It's clear I'm passionate about fashion; tell me about your latest passion.

PS. My ongoing passion is taking photographs—which I do most days. Recently I have been shooting for my own advertising campaign and also working doing fashion and interior shoots for various magazines, such as *Numero* in Japan, *L'Express* and *Stiletto* in France, and *Grazia Casa* and *D la Repubblica* in Italy.

FL. What is "style" to you?

PS. Something that comes naturally and is not forced and definitely not about buying an expensive designer outfit. You can look stylish wearing clothes from a charity shop or borrowed from your mum; it's about the way you wear them.

FL. I need to make a serious impression and show I can be trusted absolutely to make sensible decisions. What shall I wear today?

PS. I'd suggest look 29, from A/W '10—a lilac organza big bud print circular shawl dress over a big tulle underskirt to give it volume. Wear it with a lilac fine mohair cardigan and red leather ankle boots.

I love the poor little rich girl look,
he won't be able to resist!
Thank you.
bunny kisses
fifi lapin
xxx

fifi lapin

WHAT SHALL I WEAR TODAY?

Thank You!

First and foremost, I would like to thank all the fantastic designers
who took part in this book, who continue to amaze,
and without whom, let's face it, I would be naked.

Special thanks go to Eley Kishimoto, Emma Hill, Barbara Hulanicki,
Michael van der Ham, Erdem, Anna Sui, and Paul Smith for giving
their time and helping me answer that enduring question,
"What shall I wear today?"

I would like to thank Daddy for allowing me to have a wardrobe that
is the envy of the world and Mother for passing on her style genes—
heaven knows where I would be without them.

Thank you to Sonny Hare for putting up with my biggest
tantrum to date when my gold card was refused.

To Ruby, for always being a shoulder to cry on and for selflessly
taking the excess of my bulging wardrobe off my paws.

To Stella, always there with a happy tail to persuade
me away from my work for a sniff around the park.

And finally to my darling editor Jocasta and to Camilla,
for all their hard work and support.

Acknowledgments

The publishers would like to thank all the fashion designers who generously gave permission for their designs to be included in this book.

Courtesy Peter Som: 4, 16. Courtesy Burberry/ photo © firstview.com: 4. © firstview.com: 19, 22, 55, 91, 109 (bottom), 112 (top), 127 (bottom). Courtesy Marc by Marc Jacobs: 23, 130. Courtesy Paul Smith: 23, 134–137. Courtesy Phillip Lim/ photo © firstview.com: 23, 37, 130. Courtesy Eley Kishimoto: 29 (middle and bottom), 41, 112, photo © Kumi Saito: 28, 31, photo © David Grandorge 6A Architects: 29 (top), photo © Richard H Smith London 6A Architects: 30. Courtesy Karen Walker: 34. Courtesy William Rast/ photo © firstview.com: 36. Courtesy Cynthia Rowley: 37, 108. Courtesy Missoni: 40. Courtesy Richard Nicoll/ photo © firstview.com: 40. Courtesy Charles Anastase: 41, 77, 127. Courtesy Lacoste/ photo © firstview.com: 41. Courtesy Mulberry: 47–49, photo © Venetia Dearden: 46. Courtesy Marc Jacobs: 52, 126. Courtesy Betsey Johnson/ photo © firstview.com: 54. Courtesy Monique Lhuillier: 58, 95. Courtesy Erin Fetherston: 59. Courtesy Louis Vuitton/ photo © firstview.com: 59, 113. Courtesy Prada: 59. Courtesy Barbara Hulanicki: 65. Photo © Dania Grabie: 64. Photo © Hulton Archive Getty Images: 66. Courtesy Louise Gray: 70. Courtesy Preen: 72. Courtesy Louise Goldin: 76. Courtesy Danielle Scutt/ photo © firstview.com: 77. Courtesy David Koma/ photo © Catwalking.com: 77. Courtesy Michael van der Ham: 82–85. Courtesy Vivienne Westwood: 88. Courtesy BCBGMAXAZRIA: 90. Courtesy Alberta Ferretti: 95, 109. Courtesy Julien Macdonald: 95. Courtesy Erdem: 101. Photo © Thomas Giddings: 100. Photo © Billa Baldwin 102. Photo © Catwalking.com 103. Courtesy Miu Miu/ photo © firstview.com: 106. Courtesy Gucci/ photo © firstview.com: 113. Courtesy Tibi: 113. Courtesy Anna Sui: 116–119. Courtesy Victoria Beckham: 124. Courtesy Diane von Furstenberg: 131. Courtesy Prada: 131. Courtesy Yves Saint Laurent: 131. Courtesy Emma Cook: 143.

Every reasonable effort has been made to contact the copyright holders of material reproduced in this book. But if there are any errors or omissions, the publisher will be pleased to insert the appropriate acknowledgment in any subsequent editions of this publication.

Emma Cook

bunny kisses

fifi lapin

xxx